The Day of the Flying Ants

Emily Cotterill

smith|doorstop

Published 2019 by
Smith|Doorstop Books
The Poetry Business
Campo House
54 Campo Lane
Sheffield S1 2EG

ISBN 978-1-912196-19-7

Designed and Typeset by Utter
Printed by Biddles Books

Smith|Doorstop Books are a member of Inpress:
www.inpressbooks.co.uk. Distributed by NBN International, Airport
Business Centre, 10 Thornbury Road Plymouth PL6 7PP

The Poetry Business gratefully acknowledges the support
of Arts Council England.

Supported by
**ARTS COUNCIL
ENGLAND**

Contents

*This pamphlet is dedicated to Alfreton, even the
bits that happen in Wales.*

At Least Not in Wales

after R. S. Thomas

Come on, and move back west with me.
The bright girls from the valleys will say
they can't hear the difference in English accents,
I won't know if they are lying, but I'll laugh.
Maybe in Cymru we can match – until I split myself
down an unforgettable seam, to show them
coal dust in my lungs, blackened blood matching theirs,
the threat of a red brick still hanging in the air.
England forces itself between each of us
and you cannot live in the present.

They Don't Come in Tins

In 1999, as far from the sea as you can get
with your feet on a playground in England,
a banana boat is the thing Auntie Rowena
fell from on holiday, rupturing an ear drum.
I am not allowed to ride on banana boats and so
I am jealous of the man in the corner shop,
putting twenty-seven pence stickers on crisps
from a multipack box because he came in on one.
It takes an embarrassment of years to realise.
I read the labels in Tesco, Lidl and Asda,
Britain's bananas have never seen Pakistan.

'Bindi'

At the beginning of Brownies in the bowls hall,
I sit opposite Charlotte in the misshapen circle of
small white girls with culottes and crossed legs.
She has pressed a diamanté sticker into the centre
of her forehead, as we pass the news around she calls it
a bindi. The real ones, she says, are pressed in with a pin.
She is two years older, I have no reason not to believe her.
In my bedroom is a Minnie Mouse pin badge with
a rubber butterfly back, sometimes I press it into
the soft skin inside my nose, jealous of boys who duck out
of lessons with blood dripping onto their wobbling teeth.
People do these things. That night, instead, I put it flush
to the flat bone above my nose, mark out a monobrow
from this excessively Western memorabilia, marvel
at the might of these new warlike women. I fear them.

Footpath to Shining Cliff Woods

Grass grows back over soft tyre tracks.
This year, of course, the road is louder
but for the sake of a girl, a dog and a father,
all sound disappears. We are invading history,
rewilding our own biology.

Every year a piece of flora takes back over:
corrugated iron crumbles, orange dust on
a cracked concrete floor. When I was a child
I think I knew what this factory was for but now,
it invites archaeology. The mushrooms sprout,
blackberries stain our faces and this year
there are more sweet chestnuts
than we ever gathered before.

Early on we crush their cases in damp leaves,
encouraging the compost with our plastic heels
but when the sun begins to set we bend,
lowering the weight on aching hind legs
and pry apart tiny presents, hardened fingers,
feeble spines.

I throw the dog a stick through an empty window –
one year, not far from now, the collie dashes in,
and an ancient wolf stalks out.

In Mablethorpe

All the pubs have two rooms: lounge bar and a saloon,
with plastic chairs and smoke hanging dense in unlocked air.
Our man comes back from the bar, decants two sickly red VKs
into empty tuck shop cherryades and we have cracked it –
underage drinking with a white screw-top lid on it.

    A square patch of foyer between the doors and
    an old fag machine, kids slipping in for Camel Lights.
    The bright music trivia touch screen and the men
    giving loud answers that blot out your knowledge.

On warm nights in the Midlands we drive right out to smell the sea.
The bone cold lingering from school nights on the same streets lifts
from the scabbed skin of our forearms. We pluck salt from the air
for our new wounds. The morning after we drive down the coast road,
clutch our sick stomachs and fly, just to see what comes from the hell of it.

The Cheeseburger Love Song

At the window is a woman you have loved against your diet,
gorged on the look of her with the guiltiest parts of hunger.
Her deft hands dance on the wax wrap paper, forearms
flecked with a hundred spitting oil scars. The fast food tattoo.
She is always here, and you suppose that she remembers you,
from her un-kissed acne years and all the warm paper bags between.
You, who would surrender your torso to the drive-thru window,
to take her by the over-washed polo-shirt collar and have her.
Her lips would have the cherry pink taste of market-stall gloss,
her mouth drenched in free-fills of fountain cola, and the thing is,
she has seen you, all of your faces in your repeated flash cars, and
she could make you in a minute. Plunge your heart and her hand
into the deep fat, feel nothing. You are ruined, crisp and bubbling.
She scrunches your wrapping. She throws you away.

Toward Mount Ida

In a too-small hot hire car we took to the mountains,
whatever the island you would drive us up its highest hill.
This time on the plastic chair standard issue at these latitudes
was an old woman, running a tiny restaurant from her personal oven.
You stooped to watch the browning surface of her moussaka,
sat under the Coca-Cola colours of the umbrella in her garden.
Later, full of béchamel and potato, you bought her moonshine.
Tucked it past customs, and in its empty oil bottle, hid it,
among the still full local spirits of so many package holidays,
between Schnapps, Ouzo, Brenevin and Metaxa – sweet Raki
with its felt-tip-on-paper don't-speak-the-language label –
a bottled travel story, eke out her millilitres at the dinner table.

Divorce

After the bomb dropped we stopped
at Tewkesbury services. You bought
your first Starbucks as a single man,
we stood in the doorway and
half under the awning,
half in freezing rain,
held hands.

The Day of the Flying Ants

When did we learn that flying ants are not another species, just another sex?

I saw us twice today while the air was thick with wing beats:
once we were children, chlorine fresh from swimming
waiting on leisure centre steps, the other teenagers,
kissing loudly with wet mouths and worried hands.

On the day the ants fly I miss our possibilities most,
remember them crawling on our bare legs?

Somewhere new queens are making their nests and that reminds me,
I should have had you, terrified, while your mum folded sheets on the landing.

Your Parents' House is For Sale

Names like ours were made for fast lives pressed together,
comfortable sharing space on the same class registers with
long back gardens running up against each other.

Miles away a name like yours will spark my imagination
but I know your cousins, they are tight along the bus routes
of fifteen well-practised and familiar hometown miles.

You meet the man you marry before you are sixteen apparently
then you leave town and by now they said we'd be wed,
but they're selling the room with your childhood bed.

The Pinxton Wakes

I never mean to come home for Wakes Week
but it happens every year.
Those bright lights, this small town.

Charlotte used to beg me
with big eyes and small hands
to take her down amongst the stands,
spend money I didn't have on trinkets she didn't need,
and to drive a dodgem for her,
until her legs grew long enough.
I am already older than I realise.

She's here now and I pretend not to see,
as she flirts with the boy she's out in the cold to meet.
I remember this, gossip from the same classrooms
where she now sits learning that moths
are not just drawn to bright lights
so much as dazzled by them.

The boys who turn on the waltzing wood
have danced back into town
all twisting charm, gold tooth grins
and muscle practised arms.

There's magic in them, like Sophie,
two months from pregnant,
four months from legal
had told me, between handstands.

She called him her 'gypsy boy'
but he was nothing of the sort,
murmurs ran through the classes,
when showmen were spotted
smoking on the tennis courts.

I could believe it if you told me
these are the boys we whispered about,
but time passes, even for magicians
and I have been leaving here for years.

Hereditament

Is roughly the word for a taxable space
in the complex mouth of our government.
Pound signs placed on kitchen tiles and
invoices sent to names that are no longer ours,
but those sticks and stones did grow my bones
and sheltered me from every weather.

There's a council account with our coins in,
cash rattled out for schools, roads and bins.
We poured our pockets into this patch of tax,
made it a place: a spice smell in its brick bones
and height marks hidden under wallpaper paste.
We took sticks to wet concrete, set down our names.

'Welfare

By the time the sign finally fell
it was several decades out of date.
Knocked to the ground by a football
booted over a low fence by a boy
who should have been in school.

They say in '88 the man sent to fetch it
crashed on the A617. So it hung on.
Over graffiti on boarded windows,
teenage lovers turned to couples married,
or divorced – tiles slipped, foundations sunk.

I drank cans carrying that brand
on unmowed grass around the back
but I was long gone for the fall.
A spectacle nobody saw, heavy letters
making holes in the concrete floor.

Joy

For a while they peeled the new skin from the slag heaps by junction 28,
set machines to what men of a motion lost to our past couldn't muster,
picked out fresh coal from the cast-offs. They did not let us heal.
It's hard to remember if by then they had put up the noise protecting fence,
blocking the sight of Pinxton and the corrugated walls of Joy Mining Machinery
welcoming me almost home, next to the spot where, in the slack season,
travellers stopped: rocked up at school with the rough glamour of strangers.
Either way – on the way back from homes elsewhere I picture those diggers,
working out the last cash from our landscape. I hope someone has stoked the fire,
my wipers twitch in anticipation of rain. There are grey skies, hard work undone
in the memories of this place all that time spent travelling has made me make up.

Dark Heart

I would marry this coalfield and go home,
lie on the chest of a covered slag heap.
I'd rest on the black bones of our bedrock,
if it would have me, broken accented back,
after I have loved and longed from a distance,
after I have had my dalliances on chalk.

We would have children of towns
sprouting back up in the raw valleys.
The things I would make are not human.
We would tend to our new economies,
soothe the scabs of hate. Something to suit it,
keep that heart in the ground for now.

I Have Loved Coal

Like a teenage girl loves an older guitarist
with a rough black smudge of eyeliner.
I have built my life on it,
screamed down decades for it,
COAL NOT DOLE – bared my soul for it
but old women gossip about the pit,
I know the world has had enough of it.

Coal – with its head full of history,
strong arms, filthy engines, heavy,
the small town sex of it.
Broken bodies, white knuckle wives,
the silence of canaries – has risen
from slag heaps and pit heads to thick air
spluttering into anyone born
late with an old miners' lungs.

I have loved coal but recently,
when I sit in the fresh place built
on the scar of my grandfather's pit,
I have loved birdsong, greenspace,
the safety and hope of it –
wind turbines, rising white beacons,
sharp armed, slicing clean paths
to a future.

Scarborough

Eventually everything washes up on our beaches.
My parents taught me that when you visit the seaside
you pull one extra piece of debris from the sand:
straws, crisp packets, plastic bottle caps. They told us
to hunt for sea crystals in the tide pools, smooth pieces
of sea-faring glass and later, my adult sister asks
what if everybody's parents had only told them that.
We would pick the coastline clean.

Litter-picking

I'm cramming my hands into hedgerows,
picking out plastic like the delicious eggs
of rare birds. I'm making a nest of old bottles,
weaving the strips that I rip from ragged bags,
rough in the bare branches of tattered trees.
I'm surrounding myself with the indestructible,
carrying carcasses until I find a trustworthy
recycling receptacle. I fawn over old brands,
excavating information from roadside ditches:
forgotten flavours of Walkers, vivid blue remains
of Panda Pops. I walk a mile out of my way to buy
a bamboo toothbrush, sharpen it into a degradable shiv.
Suffocating. I'm the thin end of this wedge.

Plenty

Next autumn I will gather the blackberries
that grow on the walk to work roadside.
I will drive to the country for sweet chestnuts,
squirrel them home from a pub lunch, teach you
to peel them into the fire until our nails bleed.
I will stoop low and gather fresh fungi, thinking
it strange that we pass the bottom rung of berries
for fear of dog or fox piss, but we eat these caps,
sprung from the damp mud of anyone's ground.
I would be ready for it when the weather comes
but then the landlord says it is time to be moving.
The blackberries rest then rot on the bushes,
we have been promised for harvest elsewhere.

The English Don't Have a Word for Hiraeth

Sometimes I come close to hammering a capital H
into the sign I have placed over this home, but then
something shifts back there where my blood is and
the bedrock breaks up under my old gums. I bleed
and mix iron with spit swilling through these same teeth.
The shape of things changes without me, shifts bricks,
and I come Home for pubs and parties on patios and
new foundations have been permitted and sunk.
I force my same worn retainer over the undulations
of this new shape, rough over fresh slicked ulcers
with my familiar tongue and have an ache of something,
the pain of home, in the re-set and release of this jaw bone.

West

It's best to re-enter Wales at dusk. Avoid The Bridge.
Dive from the Midlands into Monmouth and at the *croeso*
wind down your window, play *Motorcycle Emptiness*
to the famous air. Drive fast on the green roads,
they have little need for motorways just there.
Now gather what the English call consonants.
Cast off these new Latin vowels. Steady yourself.
If you must take the M4 into Cardiff, go slow,
mention those red trees that smother the hillsides,
to the empty passenger seat, or better yet, head west,
worrying the shape of the country until you find the sea.
Rain will fall in the mountains, and meet you there by morning.

Acknowledgements

'At Least Not In Wales' was first published in *The Colverstone Review*.
'Footpath to Shining Cliff Woods' and 'Welfare' were first published in *Cheval*.
'I Have Loved Coal' was first published (with a different title) in the anthology
A Change Of Climate.

Thanks are owed to Winchester's Hyde Writers and to Tim Stevenson for
sending me there in the first place, to Bridgend's wonderful Answers On A
Postcard women with special thanks to the inimitable Rhian Edwards, to the Tŷ
Newydd writing centre and, of course, to Carol Ann Duffy for making me a part
of her Laureate's Choice.